Authored and Designed by
Gerard Aflague

Edited by
Mary Aflague

Tagalog translations by
East-West Concepts
www.eastwestconcepts.com

GERÅRD AFLÅGUE COLLECTION
Copyright 2018

Teach children to
learn new things
and excite their
minds for boundless
possibilities.

malaki
big

maliit
little

GERÅRD AFLÅGUE COLLECTION

OPPOSITES
IN
TAGALOG

with English translations
by Gerard Aflague

slow

mabagal

fast
matulin

low
mababa

mataas

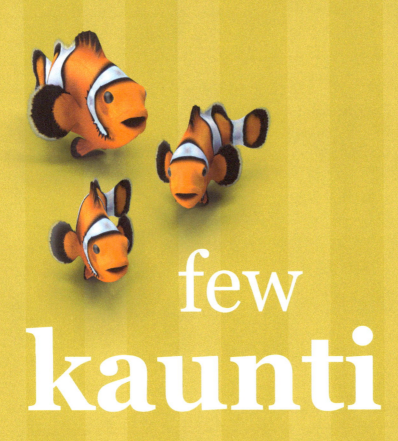

few

kaunti

many
marami

front
harap

back
likod

skinny
payat

fat
mataba

big
malaki

little
maliit

empty
**walang
laman**

full
puno

clean
malinis

dirty
marumi

nakapatay

on

nakasindi

hard
matigas

soft
malambot

smooth
makinis

rough

magaspang

heavy
mabigat

light

magaan

tall
mataas

short

mababa

here
dito

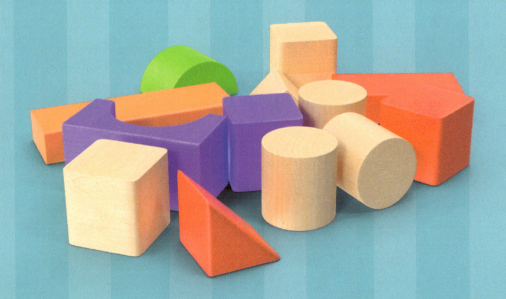

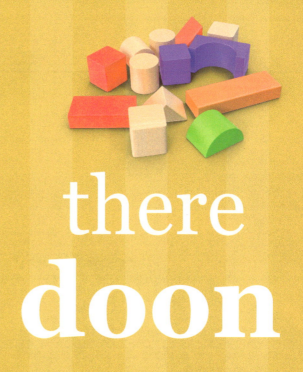

there
doon

Note: This is the term used when a person is standing at a distance from the object being referred to.

hot
mainit

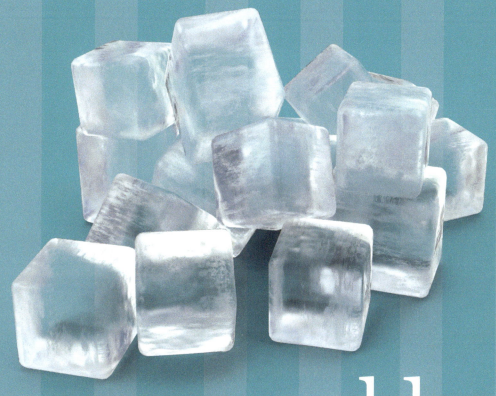

cold
malamig

left
kaliwa

right
kanan

daytime

araw

nighttime
gabi

long
mahaba

short

maigsi

thin
manipis

thick
makapal

near
malapit

far

malayo

new
bago

old
luma

above
ibabaw

below
ilalim

same
magkatulad

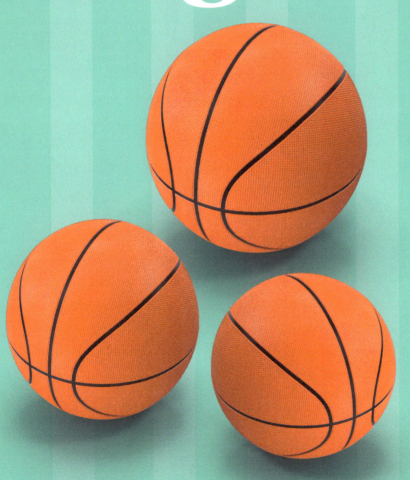

different
magkaiba

open
nakabukas

close

nakasara

The End

Actually, it's just the beginning. Go back and learn them again. In no time you'll be an expert in saying your opposite words in Tagalog!

Tagalog titles from the Gerard Aflague Collection.

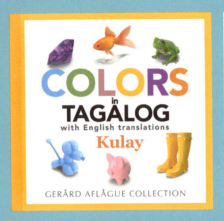

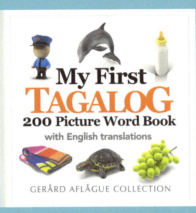

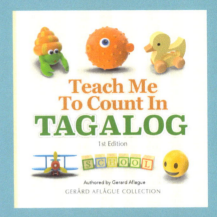

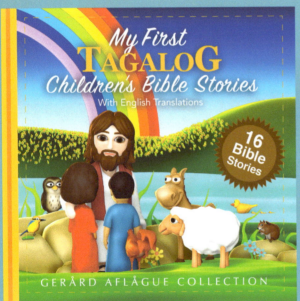

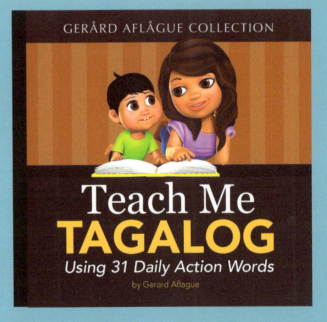

The Gerard Aflague Collection has sold over 8,000 books to date distributed across the world, and more unique titles are being designed and published monthly offering unique reading resources online. The collection also offers 750 home, office, and auto products sold on the GerardAflagueCollection.com.

Find our products on GerardAflagueCollection.com and Amazon.com.

About the Editor

Mary Aflague was born and raised on the beautiful island of Guam. Now residing in Colorado, she still manages to enjoy the outdoors and sunshine. She is a career educator in the Denver Public School district instilling in her students, the joy and power of being life-long readers and learners. Her interests include writing and editing children's books, reading, yoga, art, traveling, and Pacific Island dance.

About the Author and Designer

Gerard Aflague is a long-time Guam-born native residing in Colorado. He enjoys illustrating and developing cultural books that inspire, educate, and entertain. He also researches and writes congressional reports informing Congress about information technology issues in the Federal government. He is a passionate product designer, inventor, and entrepreneur. He also designs educational resources that are in thousands of homes and classrooms in over a dozen countries including the United States, Canada, the Netherlands, Germany, France, Australia, and New Zealand. When he finds free time in his busy schedule, he spends it with family traveling, enjoying good food, and reading a good book.

The Gerard Aflague Collection has 130+ books published to date. Many titles are bilingual learning fundamentals for children in a variety of languages including English, Chamorro, Hawaiian, Tongan, Samoan, Spanish, Tagalog, Vietnamese, Afrikaans, Amerhic, Palauan, Chuukese, Yapese, and Korean, among others. The collection includes over 25 Guam and Chamorro themed books as well. See all titles on Amazon.com.

CPSIA information can be obtained
at www.ICGtesting.com
Printed in the USA
LVHW07 848050919
630058LV00002B/18/P